GRADE 1 GEOGRAPHY:
DISCOVERY FOR KIDS

SPEEDY
PUBLISHING

Speedy Publishing LLC
40 E. Main St. #1156
Newark, DE 19711
www.speedypublishing.com

THE NATIONAL FLAGS

Color and discover the national flags of the fourteen richest countries in the world!

CHINA

USA

INDIA

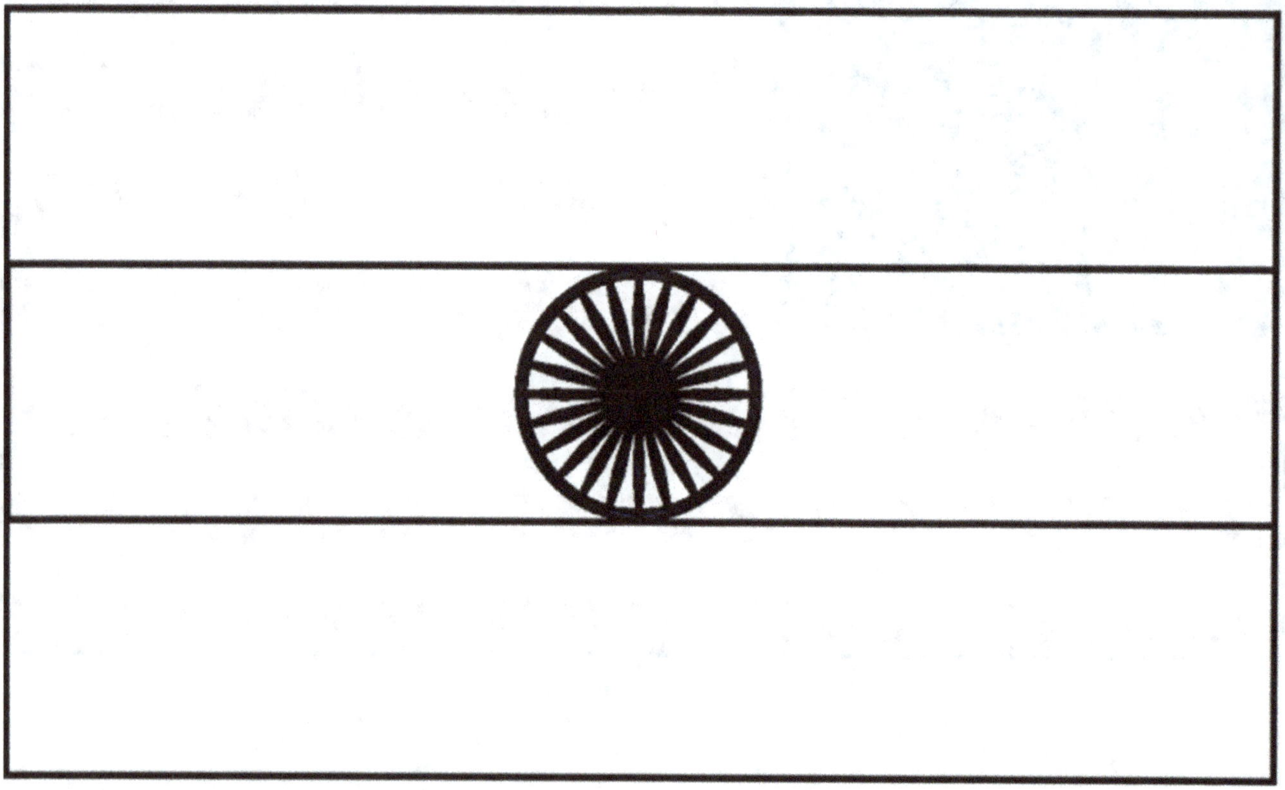

JAPAN

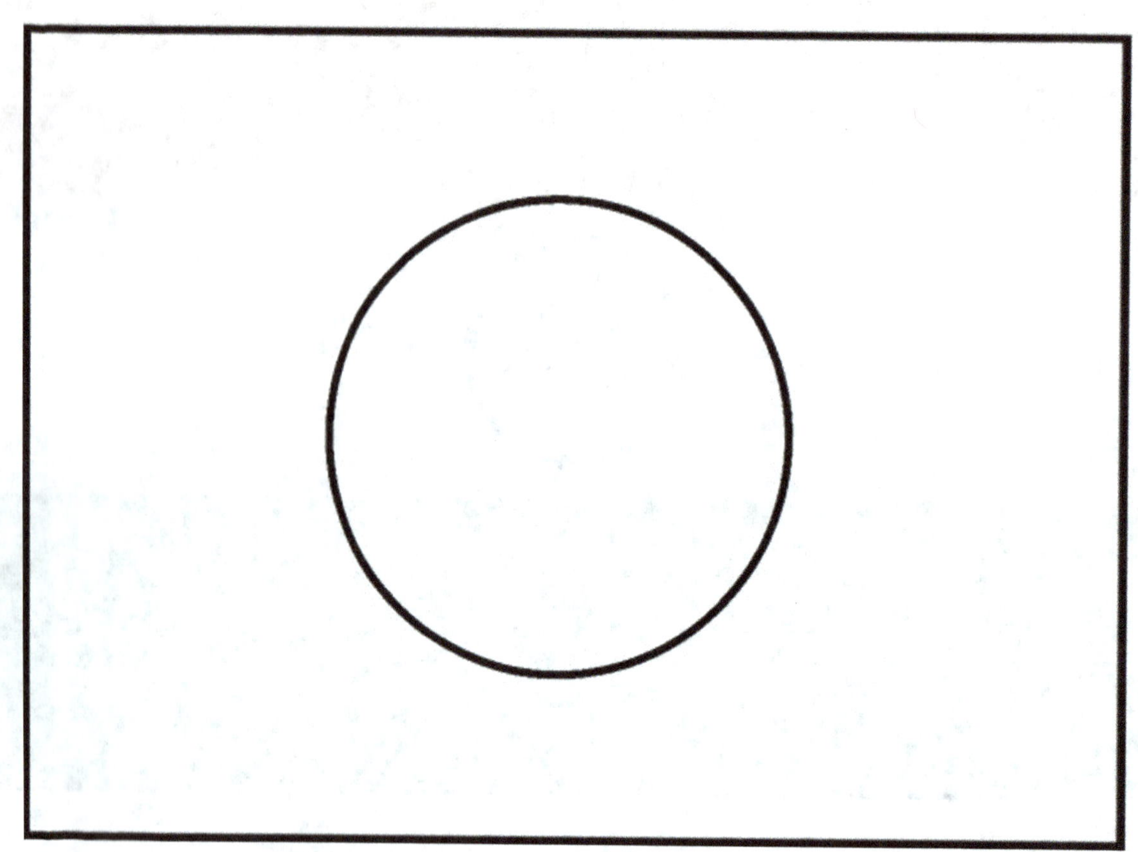

GERMANY

RUSSiA

BRAZIL

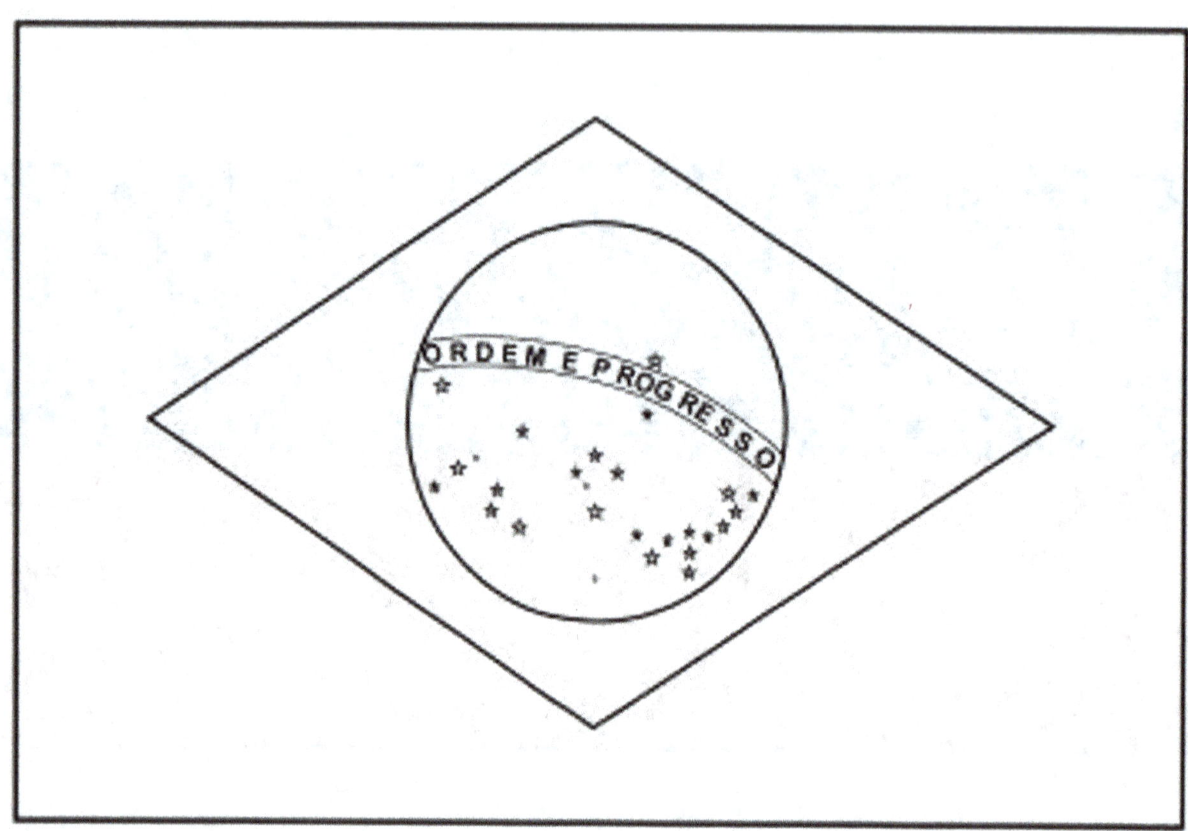

ORDEM E PROGRESSO

iNDONESiA

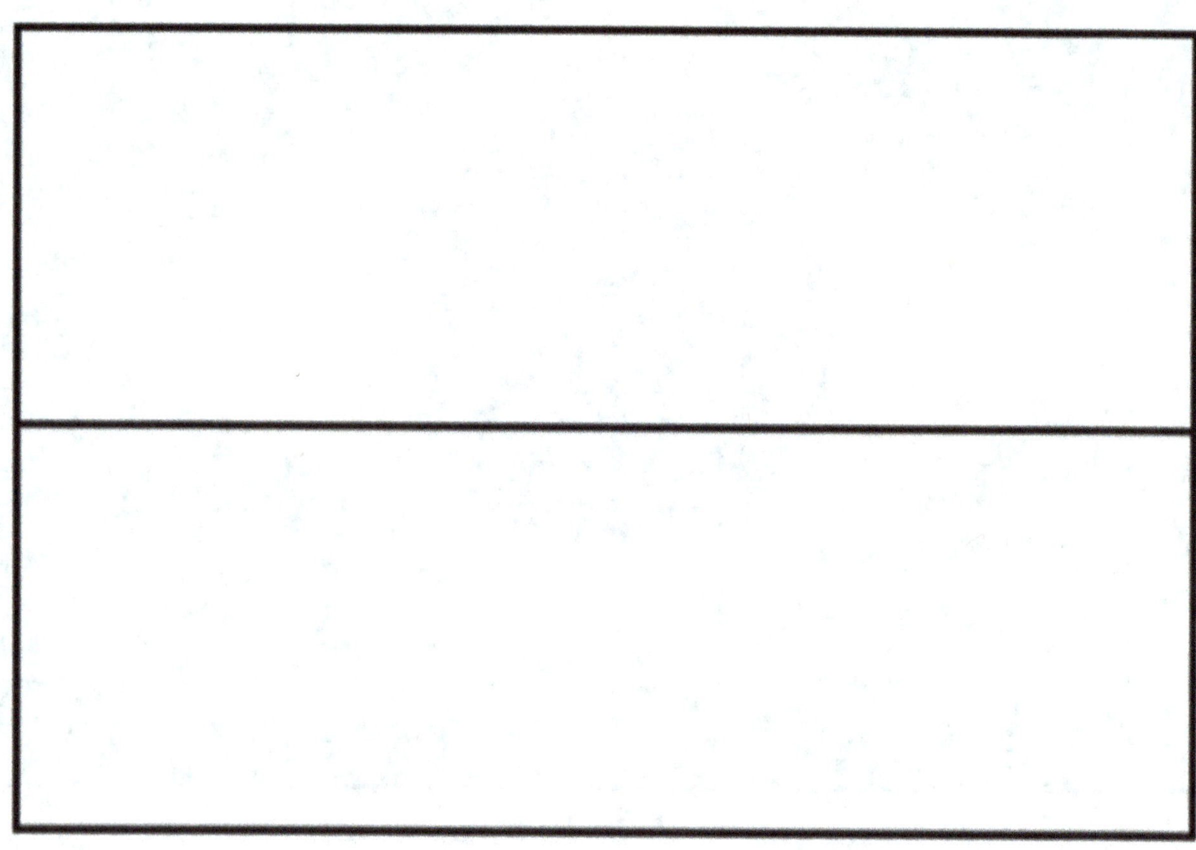

UNITED KINGDOM

FRANCE

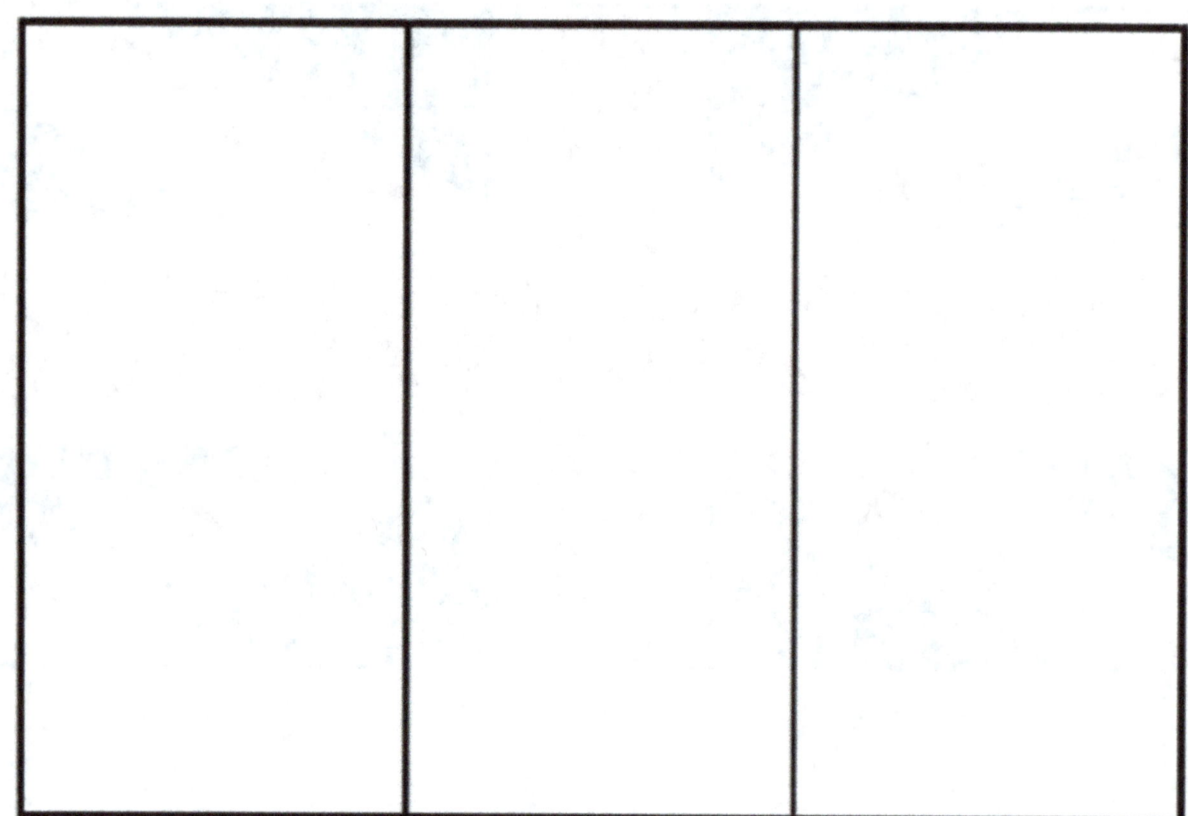

MEXICO

ITALY

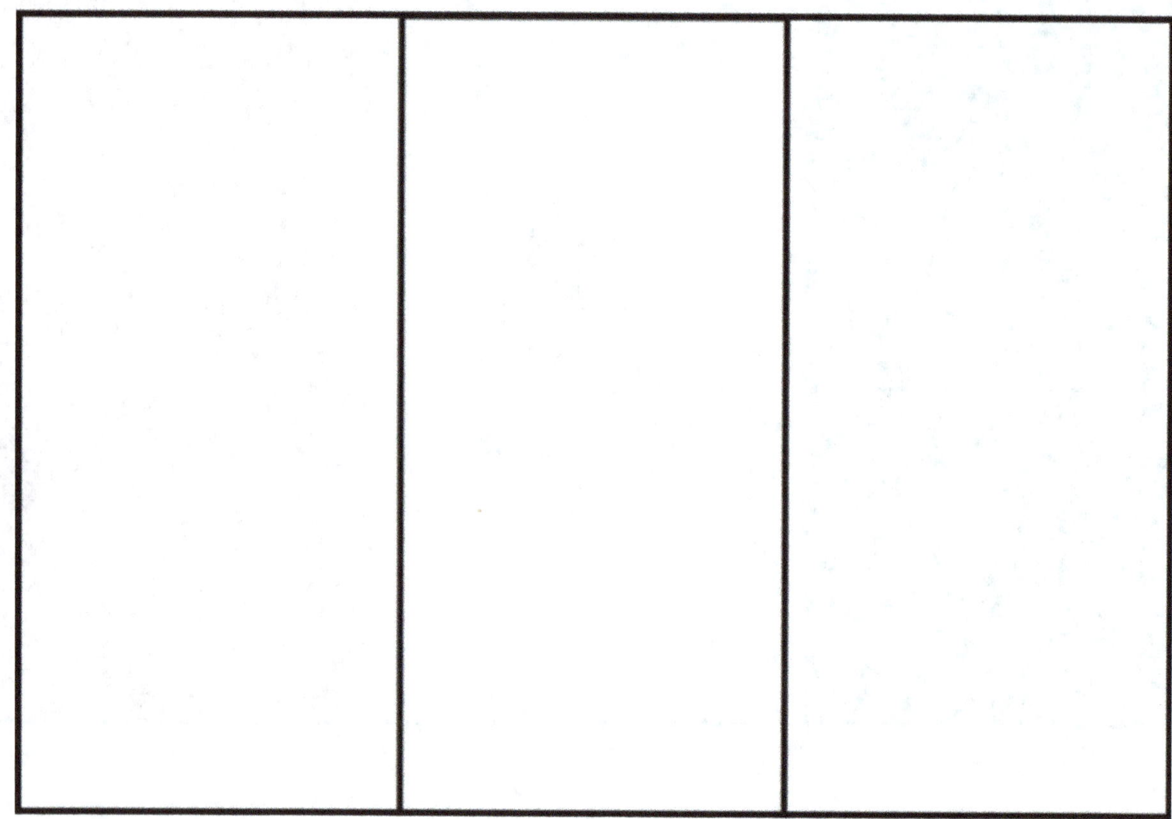

SOUTH KOREA

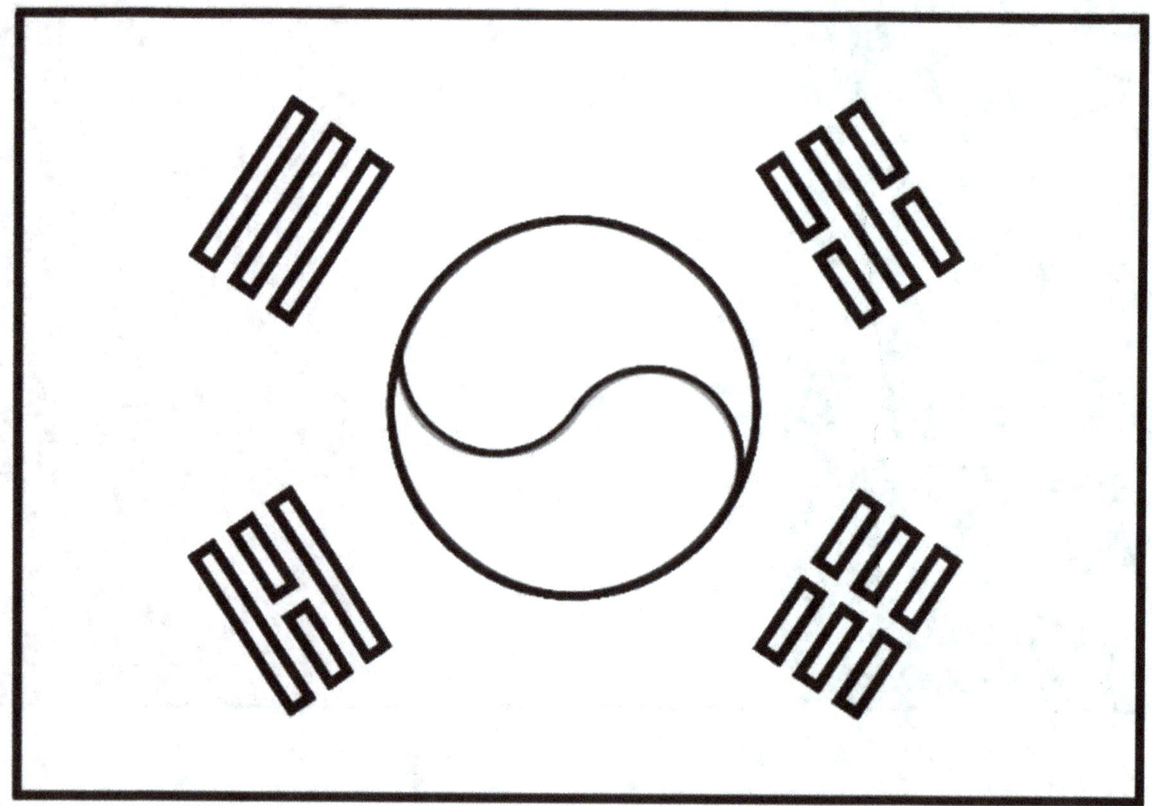

SAUDI ARABIA